So Very Rosemary

Written and Illustrated by
Annie E. J. Thorp

kregel
PUBLICATIONS
Grand Rapids, MI 49501

So Very Rosemary

© 2000 by Annie E. J. Thorp

Published by Kregel Publications, a division of Kregel, Inc., P.O. Box 2607, Grand Rapids, MI 49501. For more information about Kregel Publications, visit our web site: www.kregel.com

Illustrations by Annie E. J.Thorp

ISBN 0-8254-3846-2

Printed in the United States of America

1 2 3 4 5 / 04 03 02 01 00

For my mother,
Rosemary M. Jensen,
with love and affection

There's a lady I know who didn't always have white hair like she does now. A long time ago it used to be wild and black. That's the way it was when God first got hold of her. And this is the way that happened. When Rosemary was five, her little sister fell into a pond and sank. Straight to the bottom she went. Rosemary tried to pull Cecil out. Oh, she tried! But Cecil was too heavy.

Rosemary ran for her mama. Her mama dragged Cecil out of the water. But it was too late. Cecil wasn't breathing. Her mama didn't believe in giving up. She prayed. She told God he could have Cecil if he would only bring her back. She pushed hard on Cecil's chest, but Cecil didn't come back. Her mama kept praying and pushing. "You can have Rosemary, too!" she said.

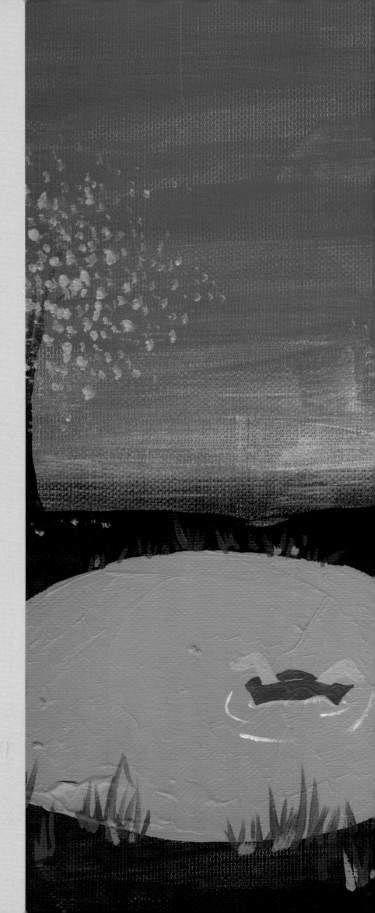

And Cecil came back, coughing and spluttering and breathing and crying, and her mama held both girls tight, laughing through her tears.

That was pretty much the way God got hold of Rosemary. She knew right from the start that her life belonged to God.

Maybe she would be a preacher. Rosemary used the old chicken coop for her church and practiced on her sisters, who sat on the chicken roosts. She preached in her best and loudest voice, the way other preachers do, but when she got older, she decided she'd rather be a missionary and go to far-off places.

She went to school and studied hard and ended up becoming a teacher. And she prayed. Oh, she prayed! But Rosemary didn't know how she would ever get to be a missionary.

One night Rosemary went to a big dance. Far across the ballroom, a young doctor saw her. He knew that she was the girl he was going to marry. Bob asked her to dance, but so did many other young men. When Bob called Rosemary the next day, she couldn't remember who he was. But Bob didn't give up. He kept calling until, finally, Rosemary said she would meet him for lunch. She did that so he would stop pestering her.

Bob asked her to marry him. He kept on asking. He carried a diamond ring in his pocket every day so that he would be ready to slip it on her finger. At last Rosemary said yes.

Bob told Rosemary his dream. He wanted to be a missionary doctor. Rosemary could hardly believe it! She was going to be a missionary!

Bob and Rosemary flew to Africa soon after they were married. Their tiny airplane landed on a bumpy, lumpy dirt field in the middle of nowhere, and Rosemary found out right away that there were a lot of things she didn't need in Africa.

Plenty of other things were different, too. She found out that going to the local hospital to have her baby was more like going to a big party. Why were all of these people trying to celebrate with her? Couldn't they see she was busy? And all the milk had to be boiled. She got used to drinking milk warm instead of cold.

Regular cars weren't much good on most of the dirt roads, and no good at all in the places where there weren't *any* roads. Bob pulled one car after another out of the mud, and even back up cliffs, with his four-wheel-drive vehicle.

But Rosemary found out there was one thing she *did* need every single day—her Bible.

Rosemary needed to know what God had to say when she helped people who were sick, and hungry, and poor. She needed to know what God had to say about taking care of her three little girls. And she *definitely* needed God's words when she nearly stumbled over a rhino sleeping in the tall grass.

Shhhhh! Don't you wake that rhino!

She needed God's words when she opened the curtains one morning and found a big snake curled up on the window sill—*inside!* And another time, when a snake slithered up the drainpipe while she was taking a bath. There are lots of snakes in Africa.

She needed God's words when she taught school. Three grades were in one scrunchy classroom stuffed with kids from all over the world.

She needed to know what God had to say, because those words from God made her strong. She needed them early in the morning, when the snow turned pink on Mt. Kilimanjaro . . .

. . . until late at night, when the stars turned white in the inky black sky.

For nine wonder-filled years Bob and Rosemary were missionaries. And then their work in Africa was done.

Back in America, Rosemary wanted other people to love God's words the way she did. She started a Bible study for her neighbors.

One day some women came to visit. They showed her some papers. They were the best notes about the Bible Rosemary had ever seen. She wanted to keep them. The women said no. She wanted to copy them. "No," said the women. She tried to buy the papers. The ladies shook their heads.

Rosemary didn't like giving up. "Well then," she said, "how *can* I get them?"

There was only one way Rosemary could get those papers. The women wanted Rosemary to start a Bible study class for them. "Okay," Rosemary said. That was before she found out there would be four hundred and fifty ladies in the class. *"Four hundred and fifty?!"*

There were already other Bible classes just like Rosemary's all across America. Rosemary began teaching that one class, but one day she was asked to take charge of them *all*.

She was pretty busy then. Oh, she was! But Rosemary never forgot her students in faraway Africa, children who came from all over the world. Didn't those people need to know what God had to say too?

She put up a big map on her wall and began training more teachers. Then she sent those teachers out to start new classes all around the world. She stuck a little pin on her map for every class.

And she kept on and kept on and kept on. Then there were little pins everywhere!

Her hair is not wild and black anymore, but she's still so . . . very . . . Rosemary.

About Rosemary M. Jensen

Rosemary M. Jensen was born in Jacksonville, Florida. She graduated with honors from the University of Florida, going on to complete graduate studies there. Commissioned as a second lieutenant in the WMSC-United States Army, she studied occupational therapy in San Antonio, Texas, where she met and later married Dr. Robert T. Jensen. Together they served as missionaries for nine years in East Africa. Upon returning to Texas, Rosemary taught and supervised classes in Bible Study Fellowship (BSF) International, an interdenominational Bible study, for seven years. Beginning in 1980, she then served as the Executive Director of BSF International for twenty years, and in that capacity she directed the expansion of its ministry from 286 classes to 971 classes in thirty nations.

In addition to initiating comprehensive leadership-training programs, she developed two additional courses of study, *The Life of Moses* and *Romans.* A concurrent school-age program was started for class members' children—grades one through twelve—that served as a continuation of a preschool program that had been developed earlier. She also facilitated the development of BSF classes in Africa, Asia, and South America, through affiliation with the Rafiki Foundation, a nonprofit corporation of which she is a founding member and executive director.

A portion of all proceeds from *So Very Rosemary* will be donated to the Rafiki Foundation, whose primary mission is to aid the people of developing nations in medical, educational, and economic enterprises, with special emphasis on providing centers for disadvantaged women and orphans. Rafiki Foundation is an affiliate of Bible Study Fellowship International.